# Vignettes

a journey through memories

## Sunil R. Nair

**Crystal Dreams Publication**

Copyright, Sunil R. Nair 2001.

All rights reserved. No part of this book may be reproduced or transmitted in any form or by any means now known or to be invented, electronic or mechanical, including photocopying, recording, or by any information storage or retrieval system, without written permission from the author or publisher, expect for brief inclusion of quotations in a review.

First published in the United States of America in 2001, entitled Vignettes – a journey through memories, by Crystal Dreams Publications / Sarah Schwersenska, Owner, Crystal Dreams Publications, 181 South Brooklyn Street, Berlin, WI 54923. USA.

ISBN
1-59146-069-7

Printed in USA.

Dedicated to my parents
and my beautiful muse - Hema

One

## Mornings

Mornings, the mists of the ended dreams,

beckoning, calling from within,

The rain, splattering a million drops

Into the expanse of the world

Awakening, the instant realization of the world around.

The chirping of a sparrow and the wetness of a pet dog's

nose.

The young golden sun drops prancing on the dew

covered sand.

Impaling itself on the tender morning glories.

Slowly coming back to the real world,

The screams coming from the yet tired body.

Each moment, movement enticing, inviting,

For another hour's sleep.

Two

# Harmony

Like the palanquin, bearing a new bride

Makes it way into a new dawn

So does my life wend its way

    Into a new morn.

Yellow sunshine, gilt edged and glowing

Aura around every person

Flute notes floating and mingling with the mist.

New rhythms born out of the morning sounds

Splashed and flung on every branch

    Riots of color invading the senses slowly,

Peace, silence and the total oneness

with my world around my aching head.

Slowly tensions flowing away

    Harmony –

The return of color,

The end of winter,

The beginning of reunion.

Harmony: my colors from a single shade of black

Passion to live life.

Three

## Vignettes of the blue sky

Like flowers in a temple

scattered at the altar

rays of light

playing truant on the waters.


Do not wipe reflections

Away form your face

The lines of old emotions

Lighted in their emotions.


Someone had thrown

The sky, overwrought with storm clouds

      in the lake.

But with luck

They turned around

And mingled with the waters,

Churning in turmoil

And what emerged is a color

That tinted you and me.


Someone must have seen

Your cry in anguish

And mixed the vast sky

Into the lake where your tears fell


Deep blue, azures like the seas

Your reflection

Unhindered and clear

In the water mixed with the sky.

Four

## The poet

Great flourishes of pen,

Staining paper in black.

Words arranged to give,

Meanings to feelings

      Touched inside the heart.


The poet

Paints verses no one understands,

Then stands back and looks on.

From a distance at the pictures.

Realizing with anger:

That what he wrote,

Is worthless in the world.


He vents his anger

Tears the pages

Sets them to flames.

Emotions turning to smoke,

And burning in the pyre

Five

## Summer has come

The purple flowers on the road
    Have come back,
Yesterday I saw one
    On the dusty mud.
In haste
    I forgot to pick it up.
When returned
    It was crushed to the ground

Wait there is another,
    A short distance away.
Surely summer has come back.

Six

## Two moths

Two moths around a flame,

Flirting in small sorties,

    with danger, without passion.

The first one dies with wings charred

    Immortalized in wax,

The second ceaselessly turns and dives

Into the shallow depths of darkness

Beneath the candle stand.


Without warning electricity returns

Drowning every nook and cranny with light.

Like a spark the moth goes

Around the tube

Clinking and colliding again and again

Trying, I think to bathe in flames

    Without much effect.

What a fool, I laugh

The first one was smarter.

Seven

## **After siesta**

Afternoons of forsaken thoughts

Residues collected in siestas

Sluggishly recollected as the milk boils,

To the aroma of instant coffee.

Returning to the earth

of highly fissured existence

A body full of cracks and tears

Stuck together with glue of hope.

Smiles return with awakened faculties.

In the joy of simply living.

Eight

## This book

This book

Is filled with waste paper,

Waste thoughts,

Waste emotions

Gnawed from writings

That ever had any time or space

To become anything.

So cloistered, has been its birth.

Now even the talk of expansion

Triggers paranoid screams

This book …

Nine

## Water

When water drops fall

Perfumed words emerge from the ground

Filtering into everything.

Into the day,

Into the mind of my tired body.

Kicking dust,

Washing away from the spot

Grime burdened over weeks.

An hour of patience

With only sun as a companion

Only a stain remains

Where so lovingly

It fell for a few moments.

Water dripping from washed linen

Trying to grow roots

In the heat of summers glory.

Ten

## Sleepless

The dawn was just breaking

I had not slept the night

Awake I waited

For the sun to burn the mist.


Through the hours

The world had slept

I had painted words

Into verses of poems


Just as the sun emerged

The pen flew from my hands

The pages turned blank,

And there were voices all around.

It was afternoon when I woke

After the sleepless night.

Eleven

## Sounds of silence

Primordial syllables of silence

Accented with the wafting breeze

From here, there, everywhere.

Basic, very, very basic.

Yet refined in nature's own way.

No notes together or similar

Everyone distinct,

Rhythmic waves of water crashing in

And soft drumbeats of hearts

Melodious in silence.

Silence is sweet, silence is complete

Mind is at rest, thoughts are vacant

Only an occasional chirp from a sparrow

And the tinkle of rain falling in a puddle.

Lulling gently into the arms of sleep.


The sounds of silence…

Twelve

## Untitled

The truth sears into my flesh,

I wait as usual for pain to pass.

Now alone without the murmur of people

Cluttering space; mentally present, omnipresent.

Lying miserable on a rock face,

sordid as the crystal drops fall in sheets.

Pungent thoughts enter through

Leaving behind debris of curses and cries.

What I had, what I have!

A truth? One measly truth,

Garnered from a miserable existence.

Without reason have weathered imaginary battles

Built within the mind,

Starved with a stomach full and tight

How often I wanted to die!

There is stench of decay

Of burning flesh

Tonight I have born again,

Purified in the heat of living.

One who talks of death.
    Seldom takes his life.

Thirteen

## In silence

Silence …

It feels like the empty spaces

Vacant thoughts, blank and foreboding.

Things that have been said,

And then a sudden gap;

All words fall silent.

Cradling heads in sorrow

Look of burdened unfriendly empathy

Voices that flow constantly

When removed leave voids

In time and in space


If ever silence were to be victor,

Let it be in final moments

When darkness covers everything

And syllables lose meanings.

Fourteen

## Death of a day

Days mature like people,

Early morning ablutions of childhood,

Faintly remembered age of youth,

And the final irony, the gift of night

Born out of the death of days.


Surprising we have lived, together

Outliving the mornings of ending days

Absorbing, assimilating, expelling.

Yet not more than having lived,

To talk of hunger.


With the death of a day

Comes sleep for eight hours

Then the return to what so ever happens

Of the newborn day, puking and crying

Remember, days mature like people.

Fifteen

## This Sunday

Ever walked ceaselessly into turns

Shacks and hutments cropping out suddenly

Where every mongrel resembles some old frail

Coughing man, both on four limbs.

Struggling to struggle, so to keep breathing.

Heavy bosomed woman, once pretty,

Now pounding clothes to the clatter of vessels

Casting appreciative looks on the beads

Strung together loosely to form a lace.


Roasted corn in one hand

Chasing flies with the other

Stepping over filth and decay

To rejoin conversation abandoned midway

By sudden reminder of hunger.

Now seated comfortably under the shade of trees,

Politics passion, violence, depravity, as time passes.

This Sunday I spent my afternoon with friends

In the heart of my city in its best garden

Across which sprawls a small shantytown.

Sixteen

## Nostalgia

Nostalgia is a bitter taste I the mouth
      Of memories gone haywire,
Lost forever somewhere in the dust
      That trails to be called time
Friends and lovers:
The simple truths forgotten
      But faintly recollected.
In the vacant hours.


Nostalgia is nothing but the past revisited
      through the misty eyes called mind.

Seventeen

# On the bus

She had come into the bus

    heaving and sighing,

hair askew, face smudged

slowly she stood balancing on the flats.

The bag delicately poised on the frail shoulders,

Pushed sometimes by the maddening crowd.


I sat there motionless, escaping through the open window

Above the rattle and the dust.

I could feel her desperate eyes

    Trying to locate a nonexistent seat.

Swaying to the slow rhythm

    Of the creaking bus.

Yet I sat motionless, like the meditating Buddha.

She was out of the corner of my eye –

Imagination grew with every movement,

Slowly she metamorphosed into a dream,

Standing there trying to dodge elbows, gropes and pushes.

She had bloomed into divinity
      in the fertile plains of my mind.


Soon she moved, her destination arrived

She trudged forward through the aisle

My eyes followed, shattered and broken.

   - so ordinary a face as ever can be,

Yet I sat motionless, without inviting her to sit.

Eighteen

# She waits

I turn and toss and think

I think of her, waiting placid

All her life embedded in the stones of the walls.

Questioning and echoing from the empty spaces

Around a simple life that she lived

She blossomed and withered,

Trying to talk and see for her,

What her mind had shown her

Dreams of colors in a black and white world.

Where a night ends, day begins:

Continuous cycles of endless hours

She waits, Staring at all the meanings that could have

been hers, she cries, unseen every night

And I turn and toss and think.

Nineteen

## The perfect moon

Beyond the bare branches that stand on the path,

The wires crossed across its face

Obscure in the smoke of the early dawn

Just out of reach.

Just above the horizon.

A small hope, in the dull gloom.

Paltry light, fighting against the streetlights.

This moon etched on the dark morning sky

Evokes gentle warmth in my heart.

The perfect moon on an imperfect day

A dream in an impossible world

The perfect moon worn out

    By the endless ravages of time.

Twenty

## **Surreal landscapes**

Spoken without words

Feelings said and heard through thoughts

One mood, nostalgic and dream like


Saffron, crimson golden hue,

Aura engulfing you in its embrace

Beauty cannot be described, like nature's whisper.


On a bridge connecting two sides,

Jasmines in your hair, sun touching your skin

     With flecks of gold.

Gentle cold breeze and ever-changing crescent of moon.


My voice seemed alien, your touch

Like the resurrection of life,
Sometimes it is better to be silent,
Let the mind take over, soul unite with soul.

The rough path disappearing over the horizon.
Time stood still, expecting so much
A lonely star in velveteen sky promising to be our beacon.

You tell me dear, could I have spoken in the midst of a dream.
Instead I let the surreal landscapes do the talking for me.

Twenty-one

## Twilights

Walked in the company

Of dewdrops falling from the sky.

Dawns and dusks

Merge in one entity


Countless birds twittering o countless boughs,

In the half-light of a dreamy sun.

Loss of sense of time and hour

Floating lightly on the air of thoughts.


Ideas half formed, lives half lived

Like the colors of a palette overflowing boundaries,

Creating mixes of shades unknown,

The end and the beginning distinctly blurred.

Have I lived?

Or has it been twilight

Neither complete, nor finite

Like dawns and dusks of everyday.

Twenty-two

# Clichéd night

Hundreds of words

Lay scattered on a hundred pieces of paper

Twisting and cavorting in agony;

Listless breathing but a corpse,

Eyes wide open and unblinking,

Sucked slowly into the vortex of nothingness.

 Up there a fan rotates ceaselessly,

Some other place the first deep snore emanates.


The rest of the house sleeps

While my window remains open,

Sending a shaft of light

To the barrenness below.

Scared, I ask a thousand times

Repeating every echo.

Am I going insane in my youth?

A gust of dry breeze

Finally wrenches the pages to the floor

Words swim in the haze

And sleep comes wafting through.

Clichéd: tomorrow is another day.

Twenty-three

## Almost unreal

Almost unreal

Flowers, fragrances and smiles.

Lost in this synthetic world,

is my innocence.

The more I try to search

The farther the path leads

Into the utmost depths.

Of stinking depravity.

Humanoid skeletons

Skin stretched taunt over flesh

Constantly floating oblivious

They are trampling my dreams

In the motion of their struggle.

Jolted out

Everything is a bit strange

Her love,

Laughter and real emotions

Almost unreal!

But I want so desperately to believe.

Twenty-four

## From down here

My foundations are built of stone.

The very ones on which stand

Generations of curses and lies

Every time I wanted to fall,

I was gently placed higher than before.

Soon I was very high above,

The reason was that I wanted to fall so often.

Then one day I decided,

To enjoy my position from the height.

Carefully standing, arms akimbo

I looked all down.

They were all around,

Chipping and breaking the stones

I bent to see better,

And lost balance, tumbling into the air.


Now I am down here

And they are somewhere up there.

Twenty-five

# One gust of wind

What bound me together,
Snapped under the pressure
And all form deserted my being
Took shape in a million moulds,
Beaten to perfection mercilessly.

One rain and I flew down,
Mixed with water to a muddy hue.
The sun took pity dried me out.
One gust of wind
And I blew away like dust,
Scattered all over the world
In miniscule particles
Each individually searching

For the spirit

That bound me together.


Even today I blow across

Your windows with each and every wisp of air.

Twenty-six

# I can't cry

Come closer to my heart; look for that chink in the Armour,

I am not what you see, I am vulnerable,

Much more than you,

I have a past all torn and patched,

Worn out with uncaring attitudes

Within me is a broken mirror

With images of blurred faces.

All loved ones, all part of my whole

The ones who turned away and walked into some dawn,

While dusk was blowing its bugle of victory in the mind.

Come into my world, I will show you the pictures.

I have no words to describe them, just

    An idea all incomplete and abstract.

I laugh and laugh and try to cry

I do not succeed, as them eyes are vacant,

Without tears, for they have flown long to have dried.

Look at my eyes, do they not seem familiar,

You must have seen them on the face of faceless millions.

I am hungry, but do I still need to ask you?

Please can't you see, I can't cry!

Twenty-seven

## As the day ends

I am silent,

As the day ends

One lamp flickers out

to let some other light into the night

you have burnt some of my sleep.


Lost, here I sit

At the end of the night

While somewhere else

Your eyes look at patterns

Your thoughts have woven.


Looked always for shores

That never emerged.

When I sank in midstream,

They born into sight

You could have led me to them.


What is the use

Of showing me

A tattered shade

Of a barren tree

When the sun scorched my back to ashes long ago.


I could never bring

Your name to my lips,

When I did,

I could not speak,

Think of anything else.


I wish I were

With you instead

Of writing this verse

So I may be assured

That you love me.


At the end of this day

As everyone sleeps,

I remain awake

Lest you pass by,

And I don't see you.

Twenty-eight

## Questions

Smoke escaping into air,

I was burning so intensely

Until the slivers of water,

From up there drenched me forever

And with them mingled my hunger

Turning common to ethereal.

Even after the many moons

Passing beyond at nights

Have explained the futility of understanding

Why I live or why I cry

Without reason,

Waiting timelessly until sleep captures my eyes

Then when the sights open

Smoke escapes into the air

In tears borrowed from the rains

Questions …

What have these books given me in return?

For all the hours I spent

    Putting thoughts to words.

Twenty-nine

## Monuments

Assimilating all that I see

And evolving to suit every circumstance

For removed for what I began as

Today I am monumental

Monumental? You might ask,

With egoism the next word to be flung at me.

Yes I am monumental.

not of cement, stone or of architectural grandeur.

Am a person standing at crossroads with myself.

Land marking epochs in lives of many

Yet crumbling slowly to meet the dust.

Two decades and ten years of living

Have somehow ravaged through my structure

Eaten away pride, eaten away innards of visions.

Old facades, edifices that you have seen

Cracking under the subtle hands of time,

So am I, turning into history with passing days.

One face of stone is my mask

Another is your memory to the world.

It does not take much to call yourself monumental

Just live in the actual meaning if it

You might suddenly discover

Your right to be where you are.

Mark your own six feet where you shall lay

To turn to dust with time.


What are monuments anyway?

Mortal edifices crashing to the bosom of earth.

Thirty

## Every moment

Every moment is an author,

Every minute a poet.

My story, my youth, my identity.


Evolution is in every step

        In every relation.

They change but foundations

        Remain constant forever

Dreams and hopes never die

        They assume new identities

Continuing their journeys.


In one small bloom is your facet

I one small teardrop is my life

Embedded like carvings on stone.

One face is what I am identified by

One face is what you are known by.


Our hands have to mature

The heady concoction called life.

Drink the potion willingly,

Breathe together, in heart of our lives.

The moments that we have are too short.


You give your precious moment to nurture it

And I will caress it, within the limits of my time.

Every moment will then be blessed with bliss.


Every moment is an author,

Every minute is a poet,

Your story, your youth, your identity.

Thirty-one

## Another poem

Search for some wound

And cry out I pain

Forgotten long back in the past.

Stand looking for persons,

People lost when you crossed

Into some other life.

Whisper some name

Etched on your heart.

The only time you fell in love

Moment by moment

Collect tears dried years back.

(You are so silent

strange knowing your nature

waiting as though

for me to carve you

into this book)


So my verses are complete,

another poem.

This one is just for you.

Not for the hundreds

For once you made me write

Not about me, but about you.


This is poetry.

Thirty-two

# The child

There is another like me

A small child

who laughed

At the mirth in living

Cried when sorrow

Overcame the burning flames.


He was who crossed

My words with blossoms,

With equal vigor flung

Rocks to make me cry,

Always mocked healed wounds

In the hope that

Shoulders would be erect
When burdens were lifted.

Then he left,
Scared away by the fear of pain,
I fear for his life,
In teaching me how to live
He lost his own way.
Sometimes I feel his presence
When I am tempted to sway,
And fall in the arms of death.

There was another like me
A small child
Now he has gone away.

Thirty-three

## Eternal

Slowly gingerly I sidestepped

Into the dawn without understanding what life is.

If one were to live by sorrow alone

Of people who come and go

One would be left gasping for breath.

When trying even to smile

At noon I realized that I was alone

With only an illusion

Of something that was called love.

Love it is said feels the soul,

So why is it that one feels empty deep down

Like some hunger not satisfied

Even after a hearty meal.


At dusk I once again looked carefully

Over my shoulder to gauge my distance

I had come too far to go back, so I walked on.


One has to die, one has to die,

Leaving behind all that is, where ever it may be.

Without hoping to be eternal, immortal.

Punctuated by a memory, photograph, and stone.


At night ... reality struck as sure as the next day

Nothing stops, not me nor the 'one',

Changing form from this to that.

Thirty-four

## **Untitled**

Don't burn my verses,

Watch them sprout into life

Take roots in the barrenness

And sway to rhythm of your breath.

If I live

I will be there by your side

And if I die

I will exist in my book.

Don't burn my verses, to reduce them to ashes,

But if ever your life becomes engulfed in darkness

Consign them to flames.

I will burn to show you the way.

Thirty-five

## Goddess of rain

Woman of winds
    In the arms of a cloud
Dreams of a summer
    Gone dull without fire.
A hundred hills scattered around,
    Fortresses, grass and weathered trees.
Patiently waiting for a streak of sun
To turn the mist in caress of golden brown.


Silhouetted against a gray blue sky
Breeze twisting dark cascades of lustrous hair
And gossamer gently suspended beyond.
Sacred, scared to touch her lips.
To break the reverie in her eyes.

The day's too short, nights too small.

A thousand years may pass by

      Rains can come and go, entombed

Within the dimensions of time

To capture her image in my words.


One goddess of rain, woman of winds

Stood in the arms of a cloud,

Watching at a distance the lifting veil

      Of a newly wed bride.

Thirty-six

## Our final destination

Amazing how life meanders

Everywhere only to stop at this point.

After carelessly having flown down

Ages, through hearts and memories.

A point where life is meaningful

Even when the vultures flowing across

The uncharted sky seem to tell words

That never had any purpose before.

From the mountains of years passed by,

Looking yonder at the visions ahead

Obscured by the mist of times to come.

As water condenses to rain

Revealing that one sight we dreamt

I slip my arms around you

In realization of one extreme reality ….

You are there by me as my life prepares

To tumble across this last hurdle

Before you and me finally merge with the seas

All the days when u walked alone

All the nights when I stayed awake

This was where our lives flowed

… our final destination.

Thirty-seven

# Raga

Yearning for touch of lightening

Waiting beneath wide skies

As slender fingers of water truce

Outlines on her contours

Strange expressions of anxiety,

Intermingled in joyous anticipation,

Fragrance in the air heralds arrivals

Happiness at knowing her beloved

      Descends from the clouds.

Dark kohl desperately his form

Ever carefully looking over shoulders

Lest prying eyes see.

Even as delicate fingers put truant hair in place.

Every syllable unspoken through gestures.

The last gust of winds clash clouds against slopes

setting up a curtain of haze.

His fingers entwine in hers,

She lifts herself from mortal to sublime.

And they evaporate into the mist.

The curtain lifts to revel the world below.

Nature shielding her until she merges

Into the hands of the ethereal.

Thirty-eight

# Wisps

Unburnt and laden with emotions,

He lays himself on the floral pyre,

Wisps of smoke escaping

From where he beheld his love

No hindrances, no empty platitudes.

Love, its sublime splendor

Love, which sees it without earthly interference

His love for her heavenly fragrant,

Where he had risen from mere mortal to divine

Love it was, he had conquered.

Vacant hours of searching amongst books

Evenings spent in mindless oblivion

Wisps, everything from mist to smoke.

Memories, staring at passing times.

Stained pages of the days behind.

Thirty-nine

# In sunlit corners

Hours spent in speculating
        Which way would fate turn him now,
Slowly relapsing into something
        Finite, a story that has a known end.
His past, the expanding meadows
        Punctuated by soft mellow grass and sharp thorns.


Smiles spreading across the weathered face,
        As he recollects the smell of first romance.
Unsure yet unconquered, the soft touch
        Of cupids first salvo.
Golden memories when she led him
        To the patter of tiny pink feet.
In winters when the tender sun

Pranced in the morning mists.


In sunlit corners of his mind
　　　Remain the memories of the days
Golden tinkling voices
　　　Gone weary with age
His past, the expanding meadows.
Punctuated by soft mellow grass and sharp thorns.
He gets up, unsteady and walks across
　　　Them to be impaled by pain.
Of thorns that remained in the dark shade
　　　Reminding him of their part.
In making the sunlit corners
So pleasant to ruminate.


His smile broadened, his walk steadier,
He walked away to meet his fate.

Forty

## Beautiful night

This night is beautiful

Dark and definite

Like some small pause

Between two sunny days.

Dreaming trees and languid breeze

Playing just outside the windows.

Moths increasingly gathering

In the pale radius of the street lamp.

Silence disturbed by the cacophony of insect noises.

This night is vengeful

Bringing back all the past,

Twisting and turning

Trying to shake the grasp across the heart

Sleep eluding, nightmare awakening

The clock strikes another hour.

Soon the sun will shine.

Then between the yesterday and today

Will be this intriguingly sad and beautiful night.

Forty-one

# Sleepless night

Long forgotten pictures

Stumbling and in my dreams.

Fantasies and laughter

Innocence and love,

A bitter combination of smiles and tears.

Romance and roses

Visualizing her in a bridal hue.

Ornaments golden in the winter sun.

Breezes that rippled across the reflections

Loneliness that engulfed when the water mirrored again.


As I turn and twist in my bed,

Groaning with the burden of life.

A slow procession in the distance beckons

Me carrying my own coffin,

The endless hours ahead in the night

And sleep eluding me as if my way is lost.


Oh! Why cannot someone burn my dreams?

To light a path to my house!

So sleep may at least find my door.

Forty-two

## Symphony

All of me

And a part of you

Much together, like two good friends

Understanding, unhindered

Each other's thought.

My words flowing freely like thoughts
    And drenching like rains on somber day.

Your lips hesitating to
    Release pent up emotions and unsaid syllables.

So much of me has understood so little of you.

I wonder sometimes…

I wonder if you really would speak

If I were to touch your heart.

Or would you cringe and hide your face,

And feign not to hear my cry?

Why should you lock yourself

    Within the confines of your mind.


All of me

And a part of you

Having enjoyed the bounty around

The rain and the sun.

Warmth and the fresh breath of cold.

Creations of some symphony

Some colors, some starkness, some music.


Yet so much of me, has understood, so little of you.

Forty-three

## **Every word**

Every word spoken,

Every memory sparkling

      Another fresh cascade of showers.

Each beautiful drop

      That fell into my lap.

Blossomed into a new verse.

I write because I hurt

I write to cry without tears.

Ever experience

      Like a long taken picture

Remains within these pages

      Elaborating in a broader sense.

Your existence… my love

You along with them lover friends.

Each forming my self.

      From within the core.

Forty-four

# **No words**

Are there no words to describe my joy?

Words that have crowded my thoughts,

Yet escaped without being echoed by the lips

Why is it that my mind has no euphemisms to describe

the feel?

Why is it that verses have not flown?

    From the end of my pen.


Millions of verses have been sacrificed

On the altar of my books

In glory of deaths, on heartaches and loves

Endless tears have colored sadness,

Reduced to mere words by the hand that writes.

Joy of being in love,

Yet undescribed in my verse.

Why cannot I explore the vastness of my soul?

Overjoyed at having found a strand to live.

Are there no words to describe my joy?


Or have I stagnated?

By the years of unmoving silence

By the grief and the darkness

That the moving streams of joyous laughter

Fails to clear my mired mind.


Oh! Please, Are there really no words to describe my joy?

Forty-five

## Truths

The truth has died,

The flesh of insincere verses has adorned its skeleton,

The failure of emotions

From the faculties of this mind.

Beyond doubt the poet in me has been lynched.


Twice loved, twice dispossessed

The books have recorded all the sentiments

Mostly tears, some bright pages decorated with joy

Browsing through them, when fancy takes

Pictures have moved, images almost life like.


In the past months,

Emptiness has replaced that fertility

The heart sets out to write and the mind

        Wanders beyond some nether world.

Inspired by a face, let down by the noise

This person yearns to be alone.


Escape used to be these books.

Where I could lose myself in words.

Escape from magnified sorrows, hallucinations;

Into this printed matter

With this pen for stoic company.

Forty-six

## Celebration

Have you ever noticed?

Tiny droplets of rain dripping off in rivulets

Washing leaves with new life

Or the delicate touch of sunshine

Bursting in a celebration at the horizon.


All throughout it had been stormy

And now the shores are near

You must have noticed the laugh lines,

Newly emerging like the smile of a new born.

Happiness not born out of words.


Without so much as a whisper

Color and life have emerged,

Fresh, with out fatigue of unwanted burdens

Only joy and warmth

Not a trace of blurred images of yesterday.

Then finally,

Have you noticed, the tiny yellow flowers

Those constantly fly in our midst

When our talks get weary,

There is joy like you had said,

Only I had to search to find it.

Forty-seven

## Journey out of wilderness

There is a small rivulet
    In everyman's mind,
        Which yearns to flow across barriers.
Laden with events and time
    Marauding all through its waters: turbid and
turbulent
In slow motion it tumbles out
    Over restraining embankments and tears
    Down emotions.
Waters washing away all traces
    Of life that was redundant with fear, without love.
Stagnant waters it is said
    Stales with the passage of days and evaporates
into air.

With no holds to stop now, the quaking tumbling slivers of freshness rejoices.

As bursting forth from beneath rocks.

    As springs, that rivulet prances and

        Cuts into rocks.

With age and maturity on its side

    As a river bedecked in the fineries of a bride.

The water cascades over her beloved mountain, emptying all her burdens.

Onto his shoulders an falls as mist

    On his stony face.

Etching on the rugged featureless mass

    A story of the rivulets loves.


This journey across so much tribulation

    To meet and change, bring to life once again

A journey our of wilderness,

    Everyman has to live by it to reach out.

And on the other side are

    The people, persons who change the tide.

Making a small rivulet

       Into a dream river with so much of desire.


There is divinity in everyman

       But only the touch of the divine

       Can release it.

Forty-eight

# Rains

Moist earth, after early burst of untimely rain

Sky is full, heavy with burden

Of water from a hundred lakes.

Premature darkness everywhere

No fiery sunsets and crimson hued mystic sky.

In all, it is magical.

Expecting something tangible to happen

Waiting for reason

For all tears to come rushing in.

No one has said a word

And realities have flown

Unshackled, for some reason I feel sad.

Rain brought new life

        When it washed all dust.

Now I yearn for the golden

Touch of the sun.

So my feeble mind may replenish itself.

Emotions that had shriveled in the heat

Of summers gone by.

Forty-nine

## A journey through Kerala

Waters and splendor

Captured in deepest blue

Reflected beyond imagination

From yonder the sky above.

Barren landscapes, tilled to

 Flower, to give solace

To hungry mouths, with bread

Ground from the grain

Grown endlessly in green, carpeted

Beds; lotuses setting up the contrast

Brown, bent forward with the

Burden of two daughters.

A slow elderly bull and a drone,

The ever swarming mosquitoes.

The last of the many desires

Fulfilled. Arabian salts and the eastern mist of seas.

Tears hidden in the spray of surf breaking

    On the beaches.

Context, though juxtaposition

With the impossibilities of returning.

A vast spectrum of memories

Onto ever onwards, me

Brought rudely back, by the stern

    Streak of the truant sun

Playing on the rail tracks.

Reflecting on and again onto my dream struck eyes.

Fifty

## In the garden

Closing my eyes,

Branches of the trees

Seem to be beckoning me closer,

Into their embrace.

When satisfied with life,

Neither hunger nor thirst

How can I understand?

A distant cry, so silent that my ears fail to hear.

Over and over one whisper

Breathing gently over the music of nature,

Sadness twinge in every word.

Heavy with the velvet dew of tears,

Eyes so translucent that life sparkle in them

Yet, a gloss of death written on a worn face.

Gesturing her to move away

I continue my pursuit of verses.

# Adieus

Sunil R Nair, 2001.

sunilrnair@emarket-places.com